# A Load of Rubbish

by
David Orme

Thunderbolts

**A Load of Rubbish**
by David Orme

Illustrated by Justine Beckett

Published by Ransom Publishing Ltd.
Radley House, 8 St. Cross Road, Winchester, Hants. SO23 9HX, UK
www.ransom.co.uk

ISBN    978 178127 063 9
First published in 2013

Copyright © 2013 Ransom Publishing Ltd.

Illustrations copyright © 2013 Justine Beckett
'Get the Facts' section - images copyright: cover, prelims, passim – Gino Crescoli, Kristin Smith, Mike Clarke, Patrick; pp 4/5 - flagstaffotos.com.au; pp 6/7 - Thomas Osborne, Gabor Izso, DerHexer; pp 8/9 - Pretzelpaws, Roger Whiteway, Nino Barbieri; pp 10/11 - Dale Reardon, Victorgrigas, Maciej Noskowski; pp 12/13 - normanack, CillanXC, Con-struct, René Mansi, S. Müller; pp 14/15 - Piergiuliano Chesi, Hans Hillewaert, alex.ch, Mysid; pp 16/17 - Tim McClean Photography, Marcin Białek, Ashley Felton, Bob Vidler; pp 18/19 - Brasil2, Intsamaritan; pp 20/21 - Gino Crescoli, Kristin Smith, Matej Michelizza, Win Henderson; pp 22/23 - Forest & Kim Starr, Vberger, woraput chawalitphon; p 36 - IFCAR.

A CIP catalogue record of this book is available from the British Library.

All rights reserved. No part of this publication may be reproduced, stored in a retrieval system, or transmitted, in any form or by any means, electronic, mechanical, photocopying, recording or otherwise, without the prior permission of the publishers.

The rights of David Orme to be identified as the author and of Justine Beckett to be identified as the illustrator of this Work have been asserted by them in accordance with sections 77 and 78 of the Copyright, Design and Patents Act 1988.

page 5

page 25

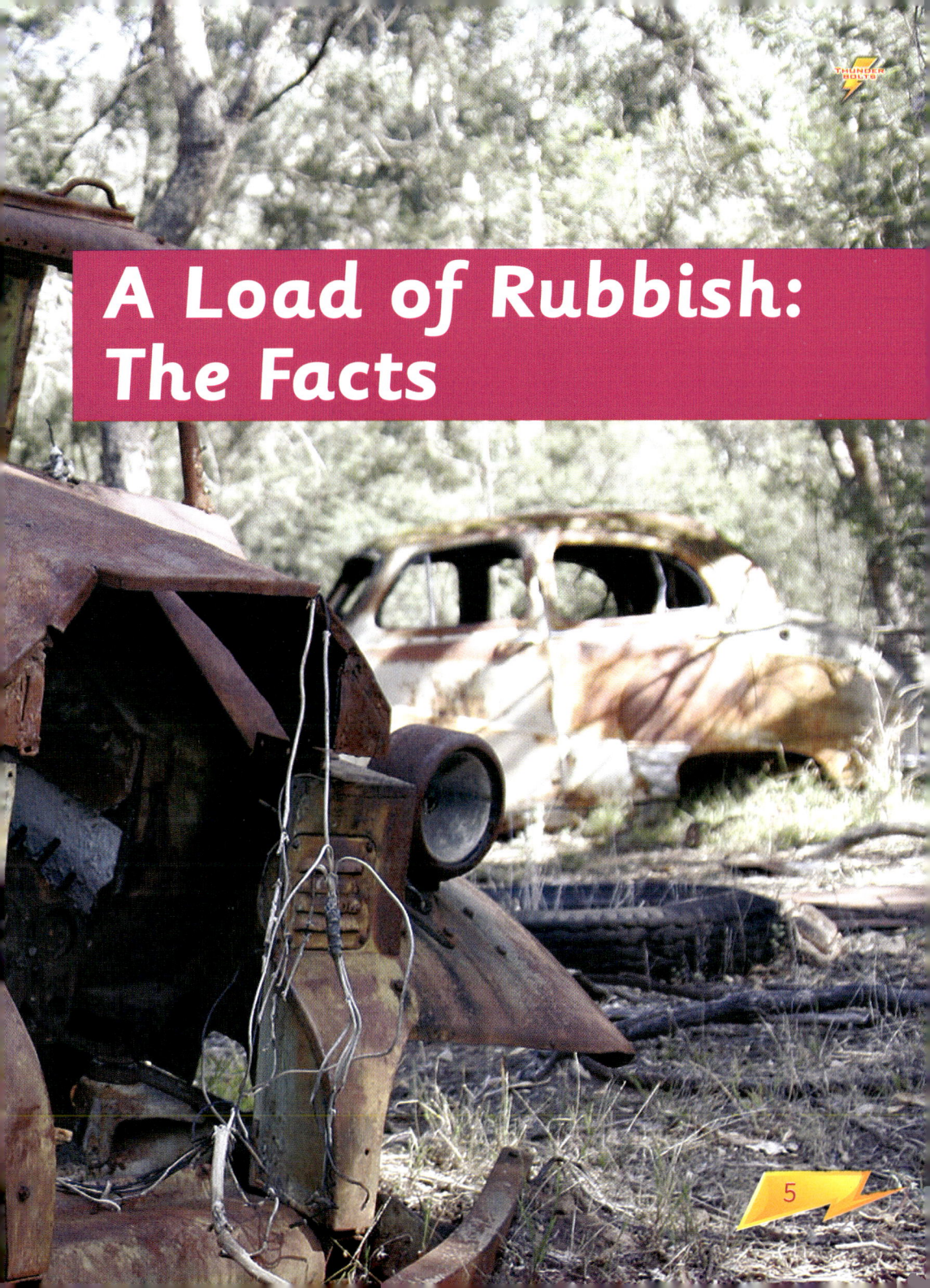

# A Load of Rubbish: The Facts

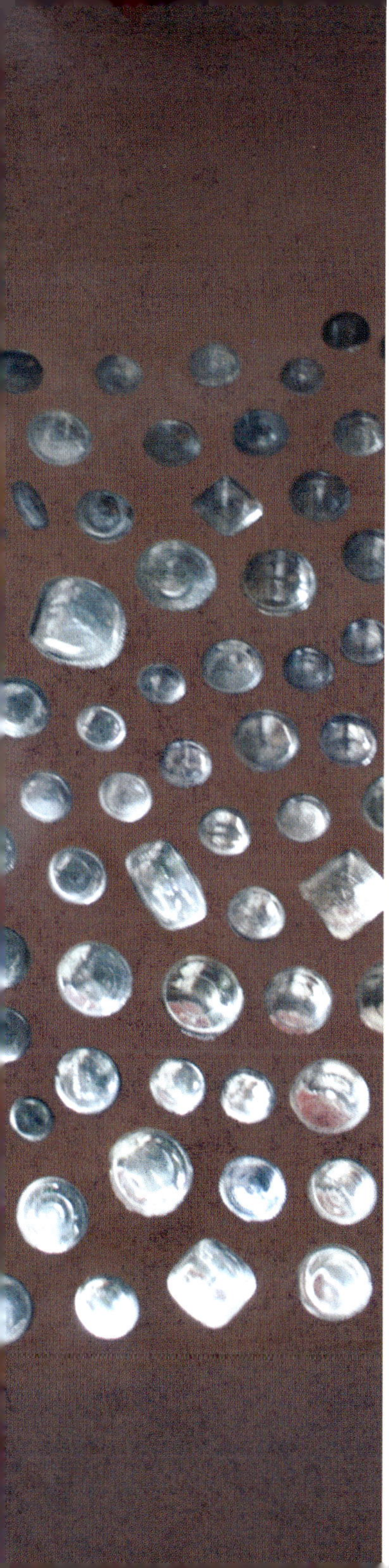